good Joy

GREAT WHITE SHARKS

THE SHARK DISCOVERY LIBRARY

Sarah Palmer

Illustrated by Ernest Nicol and Libby Turner

Rourke Enterprises, Inc.
Vero Beach, Florida 32964

Library of Congress Cataloging-in-Publication Data

Palmer, Sarah, 1955-
   Great White Sharks/Sarah Palmer; illustrated by Ernest
Nicol and Libby turner

   p. cm. — (The Sharks discovery library)
   Includes index.
   Summary: A brief description of the physical
characteristics, habits, and natural environment of the
great white shark, considered to be the most dangerous
shark of all.
   ISBN 0-86592-462-7
   1. White shark — Juvenile literature. [1. White shark.
2. Sharks.] I. Nicol, Ernest ill.   II. Title.
III. Series: Palmer,Sarah,1955-
Sharks discovery library.
QL638.95.L3P35   1989   88-4686
597'.31 - dc19   CIP
                                 AC

TABLE OF CONTENTS

GREAT WHITE SHARKS

The most famous story about a great white shark is *Jaws*. The story tells how a savage great white shark killed and frightened people on the beaches of New England. Great white sharks are the most dangerous of all sharks. It is said that they are designed only for killing. Luckily, great white sharks are not as common as other, less harmful, sharks.

"Jaws" was a story about a savage great white shark

HOW THEY LOOK

Great white sharks have brownish gray backs with pale gray or white undersides. Their **pectoral fins** are tipped with black. An average female great white shark grows to about 15 feet long. Female sharks are usually bigger than the males. The largest great white shark known was nearly 30 feet long. It would have weighed about 4 tons.

Great white sharks can grow to be 30 feet long

WHERE THEY LIVE

Great white sharks live in warm seas. In the summer they can be found in the more northern areas of the Atlantic Ocean, like New England and New Jersey. In the winter these great white sharks **migrate** south along the eastern seaboard to the Gulf of Mexico and the South Atlantic Ocean. Great whites can be found in warm, shallow bays in many countries.

Great white sharks like shallow waters

WHAT THEY EAT

All sharks are **carnivorous**, or flesh-eating. Great white sharks will eat almost any kind of flesh, whether alive or dead. They eat large fish, seals, sea lions, turtles, and even dead whales. Two whole sea lions were found inside the body of one 16-foot shark. Many great whites are found off the coast of California, where there are seal colonies on which they can **prey** for food.

A great white shark attacks a sea lion

Great white sharks are very dangerous

Some people fish for great white sharks

THEIR JAWS AND TEETH

Great white sharks have very strong jaws and huge teeth. The teeth in the sharks' upper jaws are triangular and can grow up to 3 inches long. The teeth are narrower in the lower jaws. Each tooth has a **serrated** edge like a saw, which makes them doubly sharp.

Great white sharks' teeth are very sharp

SHARK ATTACK!

It is thought that great white sharks are responsible for about 4 in 10 shark attacks on humans. They attack more often than any other shark. One-third of the great white sharks' victims die from their injuries. Those who escape are often left with ugly scars from the sharks' teeth. Sometimes they may even lose an arm or a leg. It is easy to understand why people are so afraid of these sharks.

Great white sharks attack swiftly

HOW THEY ATTACK

Almost no one who has been attacked by a great white shark saw the fish coming. The first thing they knew was that a part of their body had been snatched by the shark. Some sharks circle their **prey** before an attack, but the great white shark moves in quickly and without warning. With the first strike, it will disable its prey. With the next, it seeks to kill and eat its **victim**.

Great white sharks attack people
more often than any other shark

AVOIDING SHARK ATTACKS

The risk of shark attack is very low. Nevertheless, you can reduce even further your chances of being attacked by how you act. You should never swim at beaches where sharks are common. Do not swim alone, especially at dusk or after dark, when the sharks are feeding. Do not wear bright jewelry or watches in the water. Never swim with an open wound, the blood will attract sharks.

Never wear bright jewelry when swimming

FACT FILE

Common Name:	Great White Shark
Scientific Name:	Carcharodon carcharias
Color:	Brownish gray
Average Size:	11 feet, 4 inches
Where They Live:	Warm waters, mostly offshore but also found in surf and shallow bays
Danger Level:	Most dangerous shark

Glossary

carnivorous (car NIV or ous) — flesh-eating

to migrate (MI grate) — to move from one place to another, usually at the same time each year

pectoral fins (PEC tor al) — lower fins

to prey (PREY) — to hunt for food

prey (PREY) — an animal that is hunted for food

serrated (ser RAT ed) — notched, like the edge of a saw

victim (VIC tim) — an injured person

INDEX